What If Your
Pastor
is a
Dud?

What If Your Pastor is a Dud?

BRIAN T. JOYCE

aventine press

Published by Aventine Press
55 E Emerson Street
Chula Vista, CA 91911
www.aventinepress.com

ISBN: 978-1-59330-913-8

Table of Contents

Acknowledgments

I owe a special word of thanks to Cath McGee of Moraga for her inspiration and example, Gwen Watson of Lafayette, Rosemary Brennan of Hayward, Helen Christian and Kathy Ridgway of Lafayette, Robin Morley of Martinez, and to all who helped me write and organize this book. Thank you, dear friends, for the hours you spent on this project. I will never forget your patient love and many kindnesses. I couldn't have brought this book to light without you.

Thanks also to Greg Ledbetter, ordained a Baptist minister in 1984, who served in parishes in Vermont, and the East Bay Area. His advice and suggestions have added a great deal to this book, as well as his wonderful talents as a singer, composer, and musician at our Sunday Masses.

And many thanks to Al Garrotto for his help and great skills as copy editor and personal advisor. For example, when I complained about the difficulty of dictation with my Parkinson's, he simply said, "Stephen Hawking doesn't seem to have any trouble at all."

Foreword

I need to begin by letting you know exactly what inspired the title of this book. It originates from two luminaries in the Catholic Church in the United States today.

One is Frank Nieman, a parishioner at Christ the King Church and the Founder (1960) and first Director of the Berkeley School of Applied Theology (SAT), Berkeley, California. This program quickly became "Sabbatical Central" for priests and religious from all over the world.

The second is George Dennis O'Brien, former Editor of *Commonweal Magazine,* and president of two major universities in the United States. In addition, he was recently appointed a member of the Diocesan Pastoral Council of the Diocese of Burlington, Vermont.

The somewhat odd title comes from Frank's email to me (March 22, 2016), expressing their reactions to my recent book, *The Catholic Parish Today: Substantial, Controversial, and Uncensored* (Aventine Press). What they said came as a bit of a surprise to me, but it prompted me to write this book. Frank's message read:

> I want to tell you about an email conversation I have been having with

George Dennis O'Brien. Dennis is a former Professor at Princeton, former President of Rochester University and Bucknell, was editor of *Commonweal*, and now retired in Middlebury, VT. He published a couple of books including, *The Church and Abortion: A Catholic Dissent*.

I believe he would like to see you write sort of (a) brief handbook on what to do to turn a traditional parish into the kind you created here [at Christ the King, Pleasant Hill, CA]. His exact words were: 'I got the book. You certainly have been fortunate. We are long-time admirers of Bishop Untener, who was Fr. Joyce's inspiration. I am looking forward to reading the letters, homilies, and 4-minute offerings.

"My only disappointment was that I was hoping to get some general ideas about how to run a parish. If you have a Fr. Joyce, all well and good. What do you do with the Very Reverend Father Dud?"

Can we talk about this? Do you think you could write something? Perhaps you have a chart of a parish like Christ the King with all the ministries laid out and how each could be started? Some kind of stimulus is needed and you might know how to give it. Dennis would surely know how to pass it along. Hope you are well and thriving.

As I began to write, it dawned on me that this is a book primarily for priests, but not just the clergy. It is also for lay Catholics. My hope is that it will lead to a self-examination that will, in turn, lead to positive change. Hence, the chapters: "How Many Duds Are There?" and "Am I a Dud?"

The key to change in the Church is found primarily in the impact and vision of Vatican II, which stressed the importance of consultation with the whole Church. Actually, it means to consult with ordinary people in ordinary parishes. Personally, I have found three steps both necessary and helpful in fostering broad collaboration in a parish. The first is creative and meaningful liturgy; the second is emphasis on adult education; and the third is consistent concern for social justice.

My hope is that this book will contribute to creating parishes that are truly inspired by and modeled after Vatican II teachings, with pastors who are ministers for and with their people.

One of the best compliments I ever received came from Bishop John Cummins, Bishop Emeritus of the Diocese of Oakland (CA). At my Retirement Mass, he described me as being in the midst of my people, but not "getting in their hair."

The message of this book is that pastors matter and so do bishops

1

The Parish As a Place of Welcome

First and foremost, the local parish must be a welcoming place, a welcoming community. Again and again, the presence or absence of this essential ingredient depends on who the Pastor is.

When I look back on my ministry at Christ The King, what I remember most is that it was a place of hospitality. Whether newcomers or outsiders, Catholic or Non-Catholic, whether people came for a short visit to a funeral or stopped in to explore the possibility or intention of staying, people's reaction was above all that this was a place of welcome. Recently, when our Parish Council spent an evening in preparation for a possible change in leadership, the number one item the council members commented on was our parish's hospitality and welcome.

Having been retired for a couple of years now, it is clear to me that changes, no matter how welcome or necessary, are hard for parishioners, no matter what. Two are things going on when there is a change of parochial leadership. The first comes across as sense of welcome or hospitality, feeling at home in my parish. The second is quite the opposite: a feeling that my spiritual home is no longer home, because a major change has taken place, rightly or wrongly, necessary or not. No matter how necessary a change of leadership might be, it's going to be difficult for some parishioners not to look elsewhere and quickly move to a different parish or faith community.

When I think of the role of the Pastor and the church community, I think of two words, both beginning with "C" and both sounding negative. The first is *collaborate*. I remember growing up after World War II, watching newsreels announcing, "All collaborators will be shot." So much for collaboration! Since Vatican II, it has become a demand of the parish and all priests to collaborate with others, whether we are in strict agreement or not. I recall one speaker citing or describing the need for consultation among parishioners as an "unnatural act between partially consenting adults." How's that for a challenge to a Church called to collaboration?

The second "C" is *conspiracy*. Once again, this word has negative connotations. When we hear of someone conspiring to do something, we assume they are up to no good. But, aren't the Church and parish community a 'con-spiracy'—a "breathing together the breath of God's Spirit with and for each other"? That breathing together can only work if we truly collaborate and conspire in a parish community where everyone *feels* welcome and *is* welcome, not only, but primarily because of the presence and ministry of the Pastor.

I remember asking the late Father Declan Deane what his best remembrance was of the several different years he spent serving in Northern Ireland, during that time called "the troubles," a time of great difficulty and conflict. His response was, "What I remember most was the laughter." He also commented that, when he ran into parishioners he didn't agree with, the number one problem was that they were so humorless. It seems to me that a pastor's most demanding time is spent on building the parish as a place of welcome and doing so with humor and a smile.

My hope for all pastors is that they will remember to build a parish community as a welcoming place and that it must be spelled with two "C's"—and offered with a smile.

2

Identity of the Priest / Pastor

In a *National Catholic Reporter* article, "Pastors under pressure can benefit from 'Amazing Parish' program" (June 30, 2016), Peter Feuerherd states that "Catholic pastors are under perhaps more pressure than ever. They've been asked to lead merged parishes, often when parishioners want to go their separate ways. They are often Lone Ranger clerics, in most parts of the country working on their own with few or no other clerical help. There is the routine grumbling about diocesan directives, often sprung with little or no consultation. And then the roof is collapsing, or the heating or air conditioning needs a fix."

There is no question that today's priest, with so many pressures on him, faces an identity crisis. First of all, there is the pressure of priests leaving active ministry.

Another source of pressure has got to be parishioners coming after him armed with bibles, master degrees, and Vatican decrees. An additional source of upset is that the pastor is no longer necessarily the most highly educated member of his community. Today women religious are no longer mere assistants and helpers. They have equaled or surpassed him in education.

Also shaking the priest's confidence is the emergence of married deacons, as well as married clergymen from other Christian denominations, who are now becoming Catholic priests. Not only that, but priests quickly find or sense that the three big C's have let them down. What are they? There is the Vatican Council, the new code of Canon Law and perhaps most of all, the local Chancery.

While the Vatican Council wrote extensively about bishops and laity, it had little to say about priests or pastors. The much heralded revision of Canon Law is pretty much the same. The Chancery, described by Oakland Vicar General Fr. George Mockel at a long overdue installation of a pastor, has two speeds: "slow" and "stop." The fact is, most chanceries are projecting the corporate personality of its members and are incapable of caring or affirming priests and pastors.

Quite frankly, priests and pastors continue to be asked to do a great deal, but their responsibilities have greatly changed. Their spiritual leadership once primarily consisted of saying Mass, going on sick calls, and conducting devotions. Now, being a pastor requires them to lead community prayer and worship, but also to introduce a new brand of spirituality—not to mention seeing that the bills are paid. For some, it is a painful experience not only to watch their Mass count go down, but also to deal with parishioners' opposition and to realize that being a priest today demands a new set of skills.

"Father" is now called from parenting to collegial partnership. When it comes to community building, the pastor's role has changed from boss to facilitator and enabler. In administering pastoral care, he has moved from general practitioner, who himself provides all the service, to specialist—from primary minister to coordinator or facilitator of other parish ministers and co-ministers.

Two descriptions of the ideal of priest and the role of pastor come to mind. The first is from Delores Leckey, who for years was a staff member with the National Conference of Catholic Bishops. When asked what she expected from a pastor, she said that he needed to be a person of prayer, that he call her into genuine community, teach the richness of Catholic tradition, and preach and speak to lay people's real lives.

Another approach I have frequently witnessed comes down to telling, selling, tasting, testing, consulting, or doing nothing.

Telling can come across as authoritarian, without the pastor even knowing it.

Selling can come across as political and manipulative, usually with the best of motives.

Testing means evaluation, but the pastor still has to make the final decisions.

Consultation involves participation which takes a great deal of time and people skills.

Doing nothing means that the pastor is present and part of the group, but his nonparticipation is enormously frustrating to the group.

Clearly, the role of priest and pastor, which involves his presence and a lot of hard work, can be demanding at best, if not exhausting. Like many renewal programs today, ministry can be described as, "Christ wears out his priests."

3

How Many Duds Are There?

How many are there? The answer is brief, obvious, and painful. According to many recent reports, the single largest number of Christians is not Methodist, Baptist, or any other denomination. It is non-practicing Catholics and those who are not Catholic at all anymore! When we ask why, the most common answers are related to *parish life*. In the past, Roman Catholics have not been concerned so much with the Church and its official teaching, but with the *experience* of their own parish and its life.

For example, in the 1960s, when people were surveyed about how they felt about the pope and his teaching, many answered that they were quite negative about the Church, but at the same time positive about their local parish experience. Today, large numbers are leaving the church for a different reason. It's because of the negative experience in their local parish. In other words, because their pastor is a Dud.

Now, I will try briefly to answer the question about how many kinds of Duds there are in a traditional Catholic fashion. I have come up with three principal causes of why there are so many Duds.

Number 1: The huge growth of international priests, that is, visitors from other lands and other cultures.

This is not a big problem. After all, given our huge shortage of priests and immediate needs, these priests represent our hope and our future, as they arrive from other lands to serve us here. Language may be a problem, since they arrive from central Europe, the Philippines, Vietnam, and Latin America. In the past, that problem was easily dealt with. Language has never been a huge problem, as long as the pastor is caring and competent.

The solution is for those who do not yet have a good command of English to keep their comments short. My own mother's pithy advice to priests who had to speak publicly: "be blunt, brief, and be gone."

They also need to bring in other priests, who are fluent in English. I can't help but remember the words of one long-time Irish pastor, who preceded me at Christ the King, Msgr. James Wade (1905-1999). After arriving from Ireland in 1933, the bishop of the San Francisco

Archdiocese, sent him to St. Patrick's Seminary to improve his English, although the young priest was a Shakespeare scholar in his own right.

Msgr. Wade loved to remind me that no soul was ever saved after 10 minutes of preaching.

The much bigger problem has not to do with language, but with culture. When priests arrive with a totally different focus than what we are used to in our culture, problems are bound to arise that cannot be solved simply by keeping homilies short or bringing in other speakers.

Again and again, it comes back to the rule of the Second Vatican Council, which calls for consultation. I fear many of our visiting clergy have little experience of the values and teaching of Vatican II, but rather fall back on approaches to parish and piety, which do not fit the needs or expectations of our people. The solution is a thorough grounding in Vatican II and its official approach to how to run a parish.

Number 2: Arrogance.

At least, this is how pastoral behavior comes across to many of our parishioners, and it clearly constitutes a reason for leaving the Church. Arrogance can take many forms. We see it particularly in the way a pastor deals with women in our culture. Our own parish experience is to have many women taking leadership roles in parish life. Often, the arrogant priest is offended by their presence and assertiveness.

During the time I taught at the Vatican II Institute in Menlo Park, CA, I frequently used the experience of my own sister as a helpful example. When I was a child, my sister, who is 16 months older than I, would frequently "steal my milk bottle" and replace it with an empty one, until a neighbor noticed it and realized why I was always angry, hungry, and crying.

My conclusion based on this example is that many priests today find it hard, even later in life to relate well and work well with women because, "we are still protecting our milk bottle." I used this example frequently and publicly, until one day when my sister gave her name at San Francisco International Airport when boarding a plane. A stranger tapped her on the shoulder and asked why she was stealing my milk bottle! While the example might be a stretch, it is very clear.

Number 3: The surprising number of priests who choose rules and regulations to define the Church.

I remember the late Fr. Declan Deane who said at his first Christ the King homily, "You aren't going to believe this—I always put people's concerns at the head of Church teachings." My concern is that people regularly put rules and regulations ahead of common sense or other people's needs, when it comes to running a parish or church.

Upon retiring from full-time ministry, I received the following letter. It is also a clear example of not strictly following rules and regulations, when it comes to Church teachings.

Brian,

We have not yet expressed our thoughts and appreciation for what you have been to us these past years. So these are post-50th Anniversary and retirement sentiments we wish to share. You are a priest forever. Priesthood is the DNA of your soul and as our Pastor, mentor, and friend you have enabled us to grow in our faith and enriched our lives.

Christ the King Parish has been our spiritual home and family. Your knowledge and courage in implementing Vatican II has been pivotal in our moral decision-making. You have been theologian, teacher, social justice advocate, and humorist. You have provided us with qualified speakers and trusted us to think for ourselves. JOHN DEFINITELY MAKES SURE THAT

EVERYONE KNOWS HE IS A VATICAN II CATHOLIC!!!

A special gift that you possess (often lacking in other priests) is powerful discernment of the human condition, understanding our weaknesses, hurts, anger and joys. You were a great comfort to John when his Mother died and very helpful throughout my own personal struggles and transitions. It is very meaningful to us that you were instrumental in John's marriage annulment. Remaining a member of the Church and receiving the sacrament of matrimony was a blessing to me. Just don't forget I am one of your "oldest" and most loyal friends.

It always amazes us how you are able to deal effectively with conflict and opposing views, both regarding Church and differences with personal friends.

You never lose a friend and maintain respect from most of those who differ with you in Church matters. John loved working for you, and has never been happier (although you do at times have strong differences of opinion).

You were a great influence in John's conversion to the Catholic faith, but I, Pat, will take considerable credit also. It only took 25 years!!! What a great blessing it is for both of us to share our faith together.

We loved our friendship with Margo and all the times we traveled with you to Israel, Greece, and Italy. Our highlights of all these trips were when you gave John his first Holy Communion at the site where Jesus gave us the Eight Beatitudes. Hats off to team Brian and Margo! You certainly knew how to involve us in continuously growing ministries. No one could engage you in more laughter than Margo.

> With gratitude for
>> All you have been
>>> All you are and
>> All you continue to be.
>> HAPPY RETIREMENT!

Brian sharing the Eucharist with John Hyde in Israel.

In this case, you'll notice that I gave communion to a non-baptized non-Catholic well prior to his eventual reception into the Church. I believe it's a clear example of common sense being followed, rather than rules and regulations.

At the close of the recent synod on the family, Pope Francis made this pastoral recommendation. "The synod experience also made us better realize that the true defenders of doctrine are not those who uphold its letter, but its spirit; not ideas, but people; not formulae, but the gratuitousness of God's love and forgiveness. In short, doctrine is pastoral in its origin, interpretation, and implementations."

A second problem with putting rules and regulations before common sense arises when so many priests are visitors among us and do not feel fully at home or free to follow their best judgment, despite the present example of Pope Francis, who stated clearly, "Who am I to judge?"

I can easily imagine a visiting priest who feels that, if he does not strictly follow the Church's teaching, he will lose both his assignment and the promise of future incardination in the diocese. How much easier it was when I was first ordained. I was surrounded by priests who thought more liberally than I did. They gave me both example and fortitude to behave quite differently when it came to teaching.

I recall two examples when I found myself far more conservative then my fellow priests. The first came when I was alone for Sunday Mass at the parish in June 1963. Given the restrictions of fasting before communion, priests were not allowed to eat or drink anything prior to a Mass, including even the water that was usually poured into the chalice after communion. For the first time and quite by mistake, I had the altar boys pour the water, which I drank, and thereby broke my fast. Scheduled for the next Mass at 12:15

p.m., I decided I had to cancel the Mass entirely, until I saw crowds of people arriving. Then, I decided on a simple solution. I would proceed to celebrate Mass, but go to confession on Monday morning to confess my sacrilege. When I went to confession on Monday morning, the confessor said to me, "Get the hell out of here."

A second example had to do with a parishioner who was dying and not married to his Jewish wife in the Church. I realized that, in cases of danger of death, Canon 1047 allowed me to proceed without official permission from the Diocese regarding banns or necessary dispensations. I heard his confession and performed the marriage "in the Church," and went home proud as could be to record the event. When I informed my fellow associate what I had done, he asked me if I had gotten the promises to raise any children in the Catholic faith. This was required at that time. When I looked it up in Canon Law, I found that he was right. Technically, the marriage was not valid unless I followed up.

The next day, when the parishioner thanked me for blessing his marriage, I told him there was a "slight problem." Then, I asked him, "If by some miracle you should live and if, by another miracle, you should have children [he was over 70 at the time] would you raise them Catholic?"

He responded, "Yes, of course."

I told him, "That's all I need to know," which revealed both my conservative background and my misunderstanding of the rules and regulations, without listening to common sense!

In those days I was quite clearly a Dud but not yet prepared to be a pastor.

The author already galloping around the streets of East Oakland, intent on weeding out pastors who are Duds

"Boys who would be priests" — In 1951, 104 young men were studying for the priesthood for the San Francisco Archdiocese. In 1963, after many comings and goings, 22 were ordained for the Dioceses of San Francisco, Oakland, Sacramento, and Hawaii.

Brian T. Joyce as a graduating seminarian (1957)

Bishop Floyd L. Begin of Oakland blessing the
school library at St. Lawrence O'Toole Church (1963),
preceded by Brian Joyce in his first parish assignment.

Bishop Begin with Chancellor Brian Joyce and Vicar General Jack Connolly, with Pedro Arrupe, Superior General of the Jesuits.

Bishop Begin with papal nuncio Archbishop Jean Jadot, along with Chancellor Brian Joyce and Richard Mangini, editor of the diocesan newspaper, *The Catholic Voice*

Class of 1963 celebrating our 50ᵗʰ anniversary of ordination at St. Patrick Seminary by singing our class song, led by Don Osuna (in foreground)

Classmates John Hunt, Jerry Stanley, and Tony Valdivia dining with Tom Fry and Bishop Dan Walsh, as we celebrate our 50th Anniversary

4

Am I a Dud?

This may be the most central chapter of this book. The easiest answer to this question is to recapitulate the previous chapter in which I listed three major categories of Duds.

A fuller answer requires more time and some patience. First of all, considering the enormous growth in the number of international priests who represent our hope and our future, the challenges of language and accents hardly define who is and who is not a Dud, particularly if the pastor is both "caring and competent."

It's when we run into problems of culture, rather than just language, that we may run into the question: "Am I a Dud or not?" If a pastor has a *post*-Vatican II understanding of the Church, the possibility of the being a Dud is greatly reduced. However, if the pastor's main characteristic is arrogance, or if his devotion is primarily to rules and regulations rather than his people, the likelihood of dealing with a Dud increases. If a pastor considers rules and regulations as almost an idol, or if deals with his people in an arrogant manner, then the likelihood of being a Dud is overwhelming. Recently, I have come across a couple of Dud-like examples.

The first we ran into during a recent Easter Vigil at Christ the King Parish. Two of the twenty-one adult confirmands were twin brothers, whose mother was being confirmed on the same night in a nearby parish. The twins asked the pastor of her parish for permission to be confirmed with their mother. The answer was no. She had to be confirmed at her parish—and they at theirs! It seemed to me that the pastor's response to a simply solved problem clearly classifies him as a Dud. Talk about putting rules and regulations before people.

Another common example is not distributing the parish's song books and missalettes, "Lest the people take them home."

And the example of parishes where access to restrooms is not allowed during services.

Also, the fairly common example of not turning on the heat for the people who come to worship . . . and must stay to freeze. Then, there are places where the sound system is poor—and has been for years.

How about the pastor who spoke at length about the evils of chewing gum in church? How anyone can spend homily time on that topic is beyond me—and beyond his congregation as well, I'd bet. And, what effect does a priest's insistence on people keeping quiet in church have on true devotion and piety?

In some of the above examples, the problem is that pastors prefer to save money for the Diocesan assessment, rather than focus on why the parish exists in the first place.

* * *

If you are a currently a pastor, the following examen may help you to assess your position on the "Dud" scale.

• Have I made an effort to study and honor the history of my parish? Its prevailing culture? Parishioners' expectations of their clerical leadership? (How else can I be the lover and historian I am expected to be as pastor of his community?)

• Do I have difficulty functioning within a Vatican II Church? (This calls for a greater degree of listening, participation, and consultation than ever before.)

• Do I encourage participation in the liturgy by my own example? (If I do not participate with enthusiasm, how can I expect my congregation to do so?)

• Have I dismissed or ceased to meet with established committees, like Parish Council, Liturgy Committee, Finance Committee, and other groups?

• Have I let go of (fired), or at least ceased to meet with long-time staff members who are known for their effective ministry, dedication, and discernment?

• Do I think my parishioners (or a fair number of them) are "out to get me"?

• Is my preaching relevant to the everyday lives of my parishioners? Do I have the courage to ask anyone to critique the content and style of my homilies?

• Do I think it's wrong for Mass parishioners to talk and visit in the church before Mass? Do I make a point of forbidding this?

• At Masses where visitors or non-Catholics are most likely to be present (funerals, weddings, baptisms, etc.), do I publicly insist that only Catholics in good standing may receive Communion, rather than trying to make everyone feel welcome and at home?

• When I distribute communion at Mass, do I engage each communicant with eye contact? A welcoming smile?

• When I confront parishioners, do I do so in a scolding manner, even when others are present to overhear?

5

Where To Begin?

That's the obvious question to ask when you become a pastor. My answer is always the same: *Do as little as possible.* By this I mean, upon first arriving as a pastor, the temptation is to change a lot without listening first. Instead, the focus should be on listening and making as few changes as possible.

Simply by being there and being a different kind of pastor, one who listens, you will make a lot of changes without any deliberate intention. I recall talking to a pastor in our diocese about his tendency to change everything. What he communicated to the parishioners was that they were not the parish; the pastor was. He was the church, not they.

The task of a pastor's first twelve months is to be a lover and a historian—to fully understand what has taken place there in the past and learn to love those people.

According to Dietrich Bonhoeffer, "Most pastors arrive and make immediate changes, which says to the people, 'You don't understand Christianity. I'm the expert, and you need to do it my way.'" This is an act of rejection, almost hostility. It undercuts lay ministry.

Some new pastors cook their goose right away by making too many immediate changes, especially in worship.

Bonhoeffer also talks about "honoring the Christ that is present in the community." That means discovering how the Holy Spirit has already been working in that place. A congregation may not be doing things the way the new pastor thinks they should, but *something* is happening there.

It takes at least a year to find out where the existing power centers are, build credibility for yourself, and show the people you care about them.

First, you need to establish your own personal authenticity. People will wait to see if you're genuine. They'll listen to your sermons, observe your life, and see if your head and heart are together. They'll want to assure themselves that they can trust you with the deeper issues of their lives.

I recall talking to a pastor in our diocese about his tendency to change everything and thereby communicate to his parishioners that they are not the parish. He was pastor; he was the church. They weren't.

After a lot of discussion with him about moving to his new parish, we both agreed he should make no major changes when he first arrived. Instead, though, he looked around and decided that a huge grove of eucalyptus trees that sat in front of the parish house should be removed. In his defense, he explained to me that he did not change any staff, Mass times, or anything to do with liturgy, but instead made this necessary and—he thought—really minor change. The deeper truth was that, by removing the trees, he communicated that there was a new sheriff in town. It was not parishioners' parish, but *he* was the church. Fortunately, he became an effective, competent, and sought-after pastor. I would still argue that his first move was quite mistaken.

When I was first named pastor at St. Monica's Parish in Moraga (CA) in 1976, I listened and made as few changes as possible. Listening involved parish meetings where people were asked to articulate their hopes for the future of the parish. Quite frankly, I knew what their number one hope would be. It came as no surprise to me or anyone else that their primary concern turned out to be a focus on our youth and young adults.

After the listening sessions, I implemented what
people were already asking for: more attention to youth
ministry. I had communicated to the parishioners
that they mattered, that they were the church, not the
pastor.

So, what do you do when you arrive at a parish as its
newly assigned pastor? *As little as possible.*

6

What About A Parish Council?

When I first arrived at Christ the King in 1988, I found to my surprise that there was no parish council whatsoever. Early on under Msgr. James Wade had disbanded the council, when it took action he disagreed with. Now, Msgr. Wade was *not* a Dud, but an excellent, deeply caring pastor. But, he was clearly a pre-Vatican II priest. In those days, it was entirely appropriate to be one.

Msgr. Wade gave us the great example of ability to change, no matter what our age (he was already 82). While he went along with many changes directed by Vatican II, he refused to go one step further. For example, while he agreed to have lay lectors, he did not allow women readers. At one point, several very conservative and traditional women asked him to change his mind on this matter. One Saturday morning they tried to talk to him about it. He refused to see them or even discuss allowing women to read in church. Not to be put off, they decided to wait outside until he was willing to meet. He let them sit there for eight hours and still refused to see them, let alone discuss allowing women lectors.

He also preached regularly about the importance of being at Mass *every* Sunday and scolding those who did not attend, whether they were there to hear him or not. Imagine my surprise when, several years later, he was so amazed at the attendance at Christmas Masses that he asked me, "How many do you think were there?" When I admitted I didn't know, he made a rough estimate which came to well over 10,000 people. His immediate response was, "Isn't it great they don't come every Sunday? Where would we put them all?"

I witnessed Msgr. Wade's willingness to change and grow shortly after I arrived at the parish. One day I returned from a sick call and found him nervously pacing up and down. He said he needed to see me immediately about something. It turned out that a family had come to see him about the recent death of a relative and had requested a cremation. I told him that had been allowed by church law since 1963. He responded that he knew that very well, but that was not the problem.

In the 1980s, the U.S. Bishops had forbidden the presence of cremains during church services. I launched into a long explanation, telling him I realized this was forbidden in the U.S., but not in Canada, Ireland, or England. As a matter of fact, you could have cremains forbidden in the state of Washington, whereas a few hundred feet to Canada it was allowed. "Isn't that the silliest thing you ever heard?" I said.

He replied, "I told them yes, because it would help make up for the many times in the past that I told people no."

The role of priest and pastor is always to say yes to the people. Too often, we say no.

Now, back to parish councils. When I found there was no parish council in existence at Christ the King, I reviewed what happened when I was at St. Monica's. There I found an active council, and I developed the process of regularly voting for the wishes of the *minority*, contrary to the views of the majority, so people would quickly come to the view that when the Council is described in Canon Law as "merely advisory," it does not mean that its primary role is to follow the wishes of the pastor, but to consider what is best for the parish as a whole.

Early on, I knew I had to change the common policy of choosing council members who represented their particular ministries, for example, Men's Club, Altar Society. Council membership by appointment rather than election distances ordinary parishioners from their Parish Council. It can even lead Council members to vote in the interest of their particular ministry's agenda, rather than what they think is best for the parish.

The council soon arrived at the conclusion that its role was not simply to follow the wishes of its Pastor, but to regularly voice an opposite opinion, if they disagreed. Even there, I quickly found that the council was made up of voting blocs corresponding to the particular views of members who represented particular parish organizations. To deal with this, I recommended a change in the constitution to exclude particular voting blocs or groups and rather to open the council to members who represented the parish as a whole. The outcome was a much larger council than was manageable, but one that represented a broad cross-section of the parish.

On becoming pastor of Christ the King, I decided to wait until we had built a solid infrastructure, so the future parish council could represent more than this or that interest group. This led me to begin by planning major ministries and focus on creating a healthy parish with a focus on liturgy, adult education, and social justice.

Monsignor James Wade (1905-1999), late Pastor of
Christ the King Parish, with Blarney

7

Good Liturgy
Before a Parish Council

Rather than starting a council, I thought it would be good to begin with a strong liturgy committee.

The key and necessary element of good liturgy is first of all hospitality. In practice, hospitality means opposition to silence of any sort, no matter how pious it might seem. When Jesus says, "When two or more are gathered in my name," I believe He rules out silence, even silence disguised as piety.

Putting in place a strong parish liturgy, required a committee to bring together all aspects of liturgical celebration: long-range planners, ushers, readers, lectors, Eucharistic ministers, decorators, and those who create the seasonal environment. And don't forget to include key parish staff and associate priests. This makes for a fairly large committee, which should meet at the very least a few times a year to discuss how the weekly liturgies are going and whether parishioner's needs are being met. The committee's task also includes planning for the future, especially the major seasons of Advent, Lent, and Easter.

So, we began at Christ the King, with an initial meeting of everyone involved in liturgy.

Thirteen priests dance in *Hello Dolly*. Left to right: Monsignor Maurovitch, Fr. Ralph Brennan, Fr. Don Hudson, Fr. Ed Haasl, Fr. Don Osuna, Fr. Joe Carroll, myself, Fr. Jim O'Connor, Fr. Jerry Kennedy, Fr. John Maxwell, Fr. Bob Ponciroli, Fr. Jim Erickson, Fr. Paul Vassar, with Rosemary Thomas.

Chorus boys in *Bye, Bye Birdie*! Left to right: myself, Fr. Jerry Kennedy, Fr. Ralph Brennan, Fr. Ed Haasl, with Gloria Manning.

8

Adult Education
Before a Parish Council

Another pastoral need prior to development of a parish council is excellent adult education. This can and must take many forms, especially within a large parish of, let's say, 4,000 families. Building a strong adult education program requires employing every possible avenue, starting with the liturgy itself.

I recommend following the late Bishop Ken Untener's call for a "4-minute Special" at the end of weekend Masses. You'll find an example in the "Two Reprints" chapter.

The *what* of Adult Education must certainly include sacred scripture. It is the one thing that will unite us together and help us look around and realize that we have to grow. By this I am referring to pastoral faith sharing around serious subjects rather than simply getting together for friendly discussions. I believe Adult Education needs to begin there and hopefully leads to issues and topics far beyond.

Adult Education must also employ the parish bulletin for educating parishioners and offering substantial material aimed at changing lives in the parish and the whole Church. The bulletin needs to be more than just a place to run occasional commercials. Frankly, I do not find J.S. Paluch to be consistently helpful in this regard.

Parish Adult Education is a ministry in which I find women and staff members most helpful in speaking to the parish as a whole. Besides finding competent and helpful women, I found speakers in nearby schools of theology and Catholic colleges, retreat centers, etc. I've also found prominent and informed speakers in our local diocese and neighboring parishes, and beyond the diocese from Jewish and interfaith organizations.

The role of an Adult Education committee is to find these knowledgeable people and advertise their events well, both within the parish and beyond.

Jack Miffleton and Sr. Maureen Viani, SNJM, Director of Religious Education at Christ the King, leading our Vacation Bible School

Sister Joanne Gallagher, CSJ, Associate Pastor at Christ the King, meeting with the Hospitality Committee.

Outdoor Mass at Christ the King

9

Focus on Social Justice
Before a Parish Council

A third important pre-parish council foundation stone is development of a committee to well represent the social concerns and teachings of the Church. I was particularly blessed at Christ the King with one parishioner from the League of Women Voters. I recommend finding a similar person with the same emphasis on voter registration, who has connections to the wider community.

The social justice committee's vision must always look beyond the personal views and positions of its membership. The parish at large needs information and courage to face fairly divisive issues. The primary concern is always to seek the values and views of Catholic tradition and keep them at the forefront of parishioners' minds. The committee does this by making available necessary contacts for everything from voter registration to pending federal, state, county, and city bills and ordinances.

Sometimes described as the Church's best kept secret, Social Justice teachings of the Church need highlighting again and again for Catholic people— whether liberal or conservative. These teachings always call us not to one but two approaches. The first is the need for *charity*, which involves outreach by the parish. The second is *justice*, which normally involves change in policy, practice, and politics.

10

Two Reprints

For me, the number one source, standard, and context when it comes to being a decent pastor and running a good parish is the teaching of the Second Vatican Council. For that reason, I reprint here two articles that appeared in my recent book, *The Catholic Parish Today: Substantial, Controversial, and Uncensored.*

The first is a "four-minute special," a practice modeled and promoted by Bishop Ken Untener, the late bishop of Saginaw, Michigan. The key teaching of the Second Vatican Council establishes that the church is primarily the people of God and not the clergy, religious, or pastors. This teaching established and directed parish life forever after.

The second comes from a homily I gave in 2001 at Christ the King Parish. It describes the foundation for all we are talking about in this book.

"The Second Vatican Council"

4-Minute Special

March 4, 2001

Before the collection and the final announcements, and the final blessing, we're going to have the first of our "four-minute specials" or, as people on sports radio might call them, four-minute drills. In a moment, when I start, you can watch me and your watch at the same time. See if I keep to the time.

The topic today is "The Second Vatican Council" or "Vatican II." There is a writer who says there are three groups who go to Catholic Churches today: Pre-Council people (before Vatican II), Post-Council people (after Vatican II), and the vast majority who are the "'What-Council?" people?

Vatican II was a gathering of 2,600 bishops, convened by the pope (John XXIII). It met from 1962 to 1965. It produced sixteen documents to fashion our best understanding of our Catholic tradition and Christian faith and our best direction for today and for the years to come.

One question might be: How important is that Council? You can answer it by asking another question: In the Roman Catholic Church, what is the highest authority? Now, all of us know that the correct answer is the pastor!! Or, at least, all of us pastors know that. The media and a lot of people say that pope is the highest authority in the Roman Catholic Church. But, that is not accurate. In the Catholic tradition, the highest authority is a General Council invoked, not always but most of the time, by the pope to address the issues of the Church.

Probably the greatest Catholic theologian of the 20th century was Karl Rahner. He said, "In 2,000 years, the three most important events in the life of Christianity were the Council of Jerusalem that decided Gentiles could be baptized without becoming Jews, the Council of Trent that fashioned our Latin Mass with the back to the people, and our attitude toward Protestant Christians (which was defensive and hostile, and they immediately returned the favor!), and thirdly, one that took place in our lifetime, the 21st of the General Councils, the Second Vatican Council that took place in Rome in 1962-1965."

What did it decide?

We know it set the revision of our liturgy by calling for our own language and active participation of everyone. It underlined the importance of Scripture for Catholics, changed our attitude toward relationships with other religions and with the world around us, and called for religious freedom.

If I were to underline two things that were most important from the Council, the first would be recovering who the Church is by saying that the Church is not, as we had slipped into believing, that it is the hierarchy, the bishops, the religious, and the clergy. The Church is the people of God, all of us. What has happened since the Council is that we have been struggling and will continue to search for authentic ways to change our behavior and put into practice the reality that we are the Church.

And the second most important thing I would list is that the Council recovered the importance and primacy of individual conscience. This was hidden in our theology books all along. It was even tucked into the *Baltimore Catechism*. But most of us didn't hear much about it growing up. The Second Vatican Council put at the top of our consciousness and at the top of the shelf the primacy of individual conscience. It said that all are bound to follow their conscience faithfully and that true religion consists, before everything else, in internal, voluntary, free, *free, free* choices. Now, that has caused a lot of confusion and growth in our Church since 1965. First of all, it calls for freedom from all external pressure and force, when people make decisions. It also calls that internally we are bound to seek the truth as honestly and as best as we possibly can.

So, if anyone asks you, "Do you know what Vatican II is?" now your answer is, "I do."

"Essentials of Parish Life"

Homily of July 2, 2000

In the coming week, we celebrate the Fourth of July and give thanks for a lot of blessings in our Land. One of them is freedom of worship, freedom of religion. So, I thought it might be worthwhile to reflect just a little big about what it is that we do with our religion, what it is that we are about. A congressman from Massachusetts, Tip O'Neill, used to say, "All politics are local." Well, I'd also say, "All religion is local." Our experience of religion, our experience of church, is local. It's not in Rome. It's in Pleasant Hill. So the question to ask, if we want to know what we do about our religion is to reflect on, "What is parish all about? What is parish life all about?" I want you to think about that for a few seconds. If you had to list two or three things that are essential to parish life, what would they be?

Just last month, I read a quarterly journal from Chicago. It had a long article on parish life. The guy who wrote it listed two things as essential to parish life. I'm going to disagree with him a little bit. So you think about, "What's essential to parish life? What two or three or four things?" I'll probably disagree with you too. So, make your list in your own minds. Here are his. He says, "There are two things that are essential to parish life, our Pastoral Care and Evangelization." My first reaction? This list is too short.

My list has four on it. Number one, basic and essential to parish life is Community. I mean, you can be a hermit by yourself, but you can't be a parish by yourself. Maybe, all by yourself you can be a saint although, I think, a pretty mean-spirited one. But you couldn't be a parish. All by yourself, you could be an isolated Messiah, which is the most dangerous kind of Messiah. But you can't be a parish. Parish is a community. It's a community of people knit together by faith and by the word of God. That's the first thing. We have all sorts of things. That's what they're about in our parish life, for example, our school, our adult education, our small church communities, our coffee and donuts after Mass. They all have to do with the fact that, number one, we're a community knit together by the word of God.

Number two. (I'm amazed the author of the article didn't have this.) Maybe it's on your list of things basic and essential to parish life. Number two is worshipping God, praising God with Jesus, usually in the Eucharist. We're called to be a Eucharistic community, not a club, not a fraternity, not a circle of friends, but a worshiping community together. So I have that down as number two.

Now, three and four. That's all I've got. Three and four are the ones the guy from Chicago used. Pastoral Care, yeah, I think so. When we listen to the gospel today, Jesus is healing this woman. In one scene after the other, it's Jesus healing and bringing hope to people. So that's what we have to be about. She touched the hem of His garment. In a way, a parish community has to be the hem of Christ's garment for this day and age. And, that's what we do in parish life all the time, our bereavement ministry, our visiting of the sick, our counseling, our St. Vincent de Paul Society, and each one of you individually reaching out to someone who needs help. That's Pastoral Care. It's the third thing we're about.

Now, here's the fourth one. He says it's "Evangelization." I wrote down "Evangelization" and put in parentheses, "It depends . . . . It depends." Think, for a moment, what you mean by "evangelization." When you hear the word, what picture or image do you get in your mind? I want to ask you that, because there is a Catholic definition of evangelization that popes and bishops and all those fancy people talk about, that's what they are referring to. When you hear "Evangelization," what do you hear? What do you mean?

Here's Pope Paul VI's definition: When a Catholic says "evangelization," this is what we're supposed to mean. "Evangelization is bringing the Good News into every level of humanity and, through its influence, not by baptizing or converting anybody, but through its influence, transforming humanity from within and making it new."

That's what we mean. But I gotta tell you, the problem is that it may work in other countries and in other languages, but, in English, in the United States of America, somebody else has the copyright on the word "evangelization."

And so, when we hear "evangelization," we think Fundamentalists. We think proselytizing, going around knocking on people's doors, telling them about Jesus and to irritate them. We say TV evangelists, TV curers, TV preachers asking for money. That's what Evangelization brings to mind for us, but it's not what we mean when we use it in our Church. A better word might be the "Mission of the Church" or "Outreach of the Church." And we find it throughout the gospels.

St. Paul, in the second reading, is talking about equality for everyone. That's one of the values we have to stand behind. Jesus talks about feeding the poor, clothing the naked, visiting the imprisoned, that kind of outreach! It's bringing values and wisdom and justice to the world. So, when we say "Evangelization," we're not supposed to be thinking about the Church at all. "Evangelization" doesn't mean, "How well is the Church doing?" or "How many people does the Church have?" or "How lively is the Church?" or "How strong is the Church getting?" It's not about that at all. It's about the world. It's about society around us, because that's the location where God's will is going to work or not. That's the location of God's Kingdom on earth. And the role of the parish, the role of the Church, is just to bring some energy, some values, some support and some celebration to the life of our society and of our world.

So, here are a few questions. Was the Fourth of July a Church event? Was the Declaration of Independence a Church event? If you mean "Evangelization," the answer is absolutely yes. Was the Emancipation of slaves in our nation a Church event? Absolutely, yes. Was the Suffrage Movement for women's vote a Church event? Was the gathering of the United Nations a Church event? Is the Declaration of Human Rights by the U.N. a Church event? If you mean "Evangelization," absolutely . . . absolutely!

The Bishops of the world met in Europe in 1970 and tried to define what it means to be proclaiming the Gospel, because that's something we're supposed to be about. Right? They said working for justice is the constitutive part of proclaiming the Gospel. If we're not working for justice as a parish, then the Gospel's not being proclaimed. Sometimes it's tough to work out what justice is. That's why we're bringing a dynamic speaker and Scripture scholar from Berkeley, and she'll be talking about the question of justice in the Bible. We invite you to join us on two Tuesday nights. Keep that in mind.

I'm going to finish with just one quote. It's from a big Church document, written by almost 3,000 bishops and the pope in 1965. I'm not big on Church documents. Here's my problem with them. I start reading them, and then I fall asleep. You know, there's something about Church documents. They've got sleeping pills built into them. But, fortunately, these great lines on the Church and the World were at the beginning, the first paragraph. So, I got that far. And it talks about what the Church is about and what we, as a parish, are supposed to be about.

Here's what it says, "The joys and hopes, the griefs and anxieties of the people of this age, especially those who are poor and those who are afflicted in any way, these too are the joys and hopes, the griefs and anxieties, of those who follow Jesus." That's us! "Indeed, nothing genuinely human fails to raise an echo in our hearts. This community—" (Roman Catholic Church, this community Christ the King Parish; this community. . .) — "realizes that it is truly and intimately linked with humanity at every level and in all its history." Wow!

So, as a parish, we are called to be gathered as a community of faith, to worship God in a spirit and the presence of Jesus Christ, to care for one another, and finally, I don't care what you call it, "evangelization" or "mission," we're called to work for fully human values and true justice everywhere in the spirit of Jesus, bringing healing and hope to people. It's the spirit of the Fourth of July that talks about independence, freedom, and justice for all. Amen.

11

What Is a Pastor?

Obviously in this book and its context I am talking about Roman Catholic Pastors, who tend to be male and celibate. However, even in the Catholic Church this is not always and everywhere the case. For example, we do have a number of parish life directors who are lay people and married and officially appointed *and* equivalent to pastors. Protestant denominations not only accept married pastoral leadership, many actually prefer it (and some even demand it!). Many Protestant denominations—though certainly not all— have also made normative the role of women clergy.

For many non-Catholic parishes and communities, the pastor is not a church-appointed priest at all, but rather is selected by the parish or congregation after a lengthy and extensive search. To my surprise I find that some former Catholics who have joined a

Protestant denomination end up longing for the days
when a bishop or personnel board made an immediate
and quick decision. Often, there is a need for direction
and decisions that cannot wait.

It's common, when pastors are called through a
fairly lengthy process, for a congregation to appoint
an "interim" pastor to provide temporary pastoral
leadership—although "temporary" can sometimes
stretch into multiple years. This happens when the
pastoral search process flounders or the congregation
needs significant healing, before its new leader
arrives. A good interim pastor will leave the church
in better shape than he or she found it and ready and
willing for new, permanent pastoral leadership. A
bad interim leader is often just a Dud, who couldn't
make it as a "permanent" pastor.

You'd think this process would guarantee a permanent
pastor who is not a Dud, but rather someone chosen by
the people and appropriate to the parish community.
However, I hear that this is not always true. Sometimes
a congregation will unconsciously focus the search for
a new pastor on either an individual who is "just like
our old beloved pastor" or altogether different than
"the last jerk we had."

It's also common for the pastoral search committee—
under the undue influence of a few dominant
committee members—to develop their own unique
personality model that is quite different from that of

the wider congregation. This can result in a puzzled congregation, when their new pastoral candidate turns out to be ill-suited to serve their community.

Non-Catholic parishes tend to be much smaller than your standard urban or suburban Catholic parish today. I've been told on pretty good authority that, for a pastor to have a small parish, he or she tends to be like a cat; they do not have the parish, the parish has them.

Another analogy is the church as "family," where the pastor is in the parent role. The implication is that the pastor is intimately connected to each "family member," as a parent would be. While that may be deeply satisfying for those members who desire a lot of personal pastoral attention, the risk is that pastor and people can become enmeshed in ways that are not healthy for either. Things can turn out to be either very good or very bad. The result will be very good, if it represents an ongoing harmony between pastor and people. It will be very bad, if the result is a congregation that does not want to hear the gospel truth from its new pastor. Rather quickly, the congregation can seek to remove the new pastor, rather than listen.

The role of the pastor remains to help the congregation grow and, when necessary, to correct the congregation whether the people like it or not. Of course, in every congregation, Catholic or otherwise, there is tension between: "Should the pastor be the congregation's slave or servant?" Broadly speaking, the pastoral slave gives his master—the congregation—what he *wants*. The servant-pastor, on the other hand, gives the master what he *needs*. What a congregation needs isn't always what it wants, and what it wants isn't always what it needs—like a child wanting unnecessary medicine.

Pastors are often brought in to be change-agents— helping to bring needed change in direction and focus to congregations that have gone adrift. But, the "how" of facilitating that change is the all-important question. The "bull in a china shop" approach always creates resistance and resentment. And it often results in the pastor being labeled a Dud . . . or worse. Extensive empathetic listening is a critical precursor to any attempt to reshape a community whose history predates the pastor's by many generations.

The role of pastor is directly connected to and parallels the role of parish, which means it has a lot to do with the life of a parish and its essentials. First and foremost, a parish is a community. The role of pastor is to make that community a welcoming place of gathering. After that, the next question is: What do we gather *for*?

We gather first of all to give praise and thanks to God, which means we are a worshipping community and concerned about our mutual prayer life, which does not mean always asking for things, but showing thanks to God. In fact, this is why Catholics consider Eucharist so important. Eucharist comes from the Greek word meaning to give thanks. So Christian worship is primarily a thank-you gathering, as Meister Eckhart taught long ago: "If the only prayer you say in your whole life is thank you, that would suffice." Therefore, one of the key roles of a pastor who is not a Dud is to help parishioners worship well by assisting their participation.

Another essential when it comes to parish life is Adult Education, particularly given the changes that have occurred in parish life since Vatican II, including new approaches to understanding scripture.

Also essential, especially today, is Social Justice. Emphasis within the parish community must be on hearing the gospel *and making a difference*. Clearly, this means that the pastor must be a person who relates well with the people and communicates with them. If that does not happen, the pastor will certainly fail.

When we talk about pressures on a pastor, I would have to include those brought about by inadequate training. I was trained to be a Priest, not a Pastor. In my twelve years of preparation, including six years of Latin and three years Greek, there was never a class on how to build a Board, nor to work with an existing Board. We never once talked about how to hire the right people, nor how to remove people who need to be removed. Despite hundreds of workshops after Vatican II about changes in the Church, I've yet to participate in a workshop on how to set salaries, conduct performance reviews, or create clear job descriptions.

Besides inadequate training, major cultural shifts have occurred in recent years. For example, the "Nones," those who claim no religious affiliation, have become a major factor in our society. This growing segment views the church as irrelevant, bigoted, and hopelessly out of touch with reality. They know what the church is against, but few inside or outside of the church understand what it is for or even why it exists. Many tried and true methods of church teaching are not only unsuccessful, but counterproductive. According to a current website on pastors today (pastorunique. com), they rise and fall on relationship skills.

Those pastors who fall do so in the area of "relationship skills." This includes those clergy who have a problem with immaturity or cultural disconnect. They leave parishioners feeling that they have little or no human connection with their pastors, either because they are unavailable and cannot be reached, or they come across as unapproachable or even judgmental. As pastorunique.com states so clearly, "If you don't know how to talk with people, you will fail."

12

Pope Francis and Pastors

Pope Francis has sharply denounced the culture of clericalism among priests in the Catholic Church, calling it "one of the greatest deformations." It must be confronted by the global faith community because clericalism helps "diminish and undervalue" the contributions that laypeople make.

The pope has also strongly reaffirmed the right of laypeople to make decisions in their lives, saying that priests must trust that the Holy Spirit is working in them and that the Spirit "is not only the 'property' of the ecclesial hierarchy."

"Evoking the Holy Faithful People of God is to evoke that horizon which we are invited to look at and reflect upon," states the pope. "It is the Holy Faithful People of God that as pastors we are continually invited to look to, to protect, to accompany, to sustain, and to serve."

Francis also states: "We are pastors. A pastor cannot imagine himself without his flock, which he is called to serve. The pastor is a pastor of a people, and he serves the people from amongst them."

"Clericalism, far from giving impulse to diverse contributions and proposals, turns off, little by little, the prophetic fire from which the entire Church is called to give testimony in the heart of its peoples," says Francis. "Clericalism forgets that the visibility and the sacramentality of the Church belongs to all the people of God and not only an elect or illuminated few."

Francis also states that priests often "fall into the temptation to think that the committed layperson is he or she who works for the Church and or in things of the parish or the diocese, and we have reflected little on how to accompany a baptized person in their public and daily life."

"Our role, our joy, the joy of the pastor, is truly in the helping and the stimulating," he continues. "Lay people are a part of the Holy Faithful people of God and therefore are protagonists of the Church and the world; we are called to serve them, not them to serve us."

Sadly, some of our leaders think they possess all the truth and that listening to others for their input or to gain more information is not needed. What a shame, and what arrogance. Pope Francis calls that attitude "Phariseeism."

It is also important to note former Archbishop Ratzinger's commentary in 1968 on the Second Vatican Council's *Pastoral Constitution on the Church in the Modern World*: "Over the pope . . . there still stands one's own conscience, which must be obeyed before all else, if necessary even against the requirement of ecclesiastical authority."

The church should be giving more time and attention to the development of people's consciences, so that they can make informed personal decisions.

13

Three Heroes

I'd like to share with you three figures who in my life helped me become a good pastor, rather than a Dud.

The first is Bishop John Cummins, bishop of our Oakland Diocese for over 25 years. What I most admire him for is the hands-off approach he showed to pastors with whom I frequently disagreed. He'd regularly affirm pastors, when I thought a reprimand was needed. How's that for being a lover and historian?

The second hero for me was my pastor at St. Louis Bertrand Parish from 1967-73, Father Ralph Brennan. Ralph was justly famous for at least three things:

1. Ecumenism.

When Bishop Begin first arrived in Oakland, Ralph affirmed him and told him we were way behind on ecumenism and we should do something about it. The first thing Bishop Begin did was to invite all the priests to a dinner and asked them to invite two or three neighboring non-Catholic pastors that they might not even know. It was a great start for our diocese and ecumenism—all because of Ralph.

2. Collaboration among Catholics.

I learned from Ralph the importance of getting together and talking together ourselves. I saw this primarily in his support of the Flatland Fathers, a monthly gathering of all the priests working among the poor in the flatlands of Oakland.

3. The nerve it takes to be strong in social justice and politics.

Ralph taught me the importance of courage when it came to social justice issues. At St. Louis Bertrand, he hosted Cesar Chavez on his way from Delano to Sacramento. He also hosted weekly breakfasts for poor children, led and sponsored by the Black Panthers of Oakland. Another example of nerve came with the many musicals he produced. When criticized for putting on musicals in the church sanctuary instead of a stage in the gymnasium, he responded by inviting

Bishop Begin to a front row seat and gathering 14 priests to sing and dance in *Hello Dolly*—even getting me to dance as a chorus boy!

My third hero has to be Margo Schorno (1943-1999), who taught me not just to be a good pastor, but how to go about it. When she joined our staff at Christ the King in 1988, I thought I knew how to be a good pastor, but she taught me so much more by not being afraid to ask people to serve and by choosing collaborators wisely.

Margo initiated many projects which still continue today. Examples are our liturgy and environment committees, also Life Works (a ministry of support to young families). In addition, she led us on travels to Italy, Greece, and Israel with groups of 50 or more parishioners, forming friendships we still continue today. What a great way to be a parish!

Pastors, it would be most worthwhile for you to consider who your heroes are today and how they shape your ministry.

Bishop John S. Cummins, bishop emeritus of the
Diocese of Oakland, California

The late Ralph P. Brennan (1928-2003) was ordained on January 24, 1953. His first assignment was as Associate Pastor at St. Matthew's Parish, San Mateo, California. This was followed by assignments as associate at Assumption Parish, San Leandro, and St. Joseph's Parish, Pinole. His first assignment as pastor was at St. Louis Bertrand in Oakland from 1967-1973.

Margo Schorno (born in 1943) served as Associate Pastor of Christ the King Parish from 1988 until her death in 1999.

14

What If Your Pastor Really Is a Dud?

Catholics have a right to worship and share ministry with a local parish that challenges them to grow in faith and compassion. Too often, parishioners' most common response when their pastor is a Dud is to leave their parish quietly and entirely. While for a given person this might be appropriate, it should not be the starting point in. Simply walking away is helpful neither for the parishioner nor the pastor.

As a dissatisfied parishioner, your first step might be to check with other parishioners and key staff members to see if they agree with your findings and experience. Be humbly open to the possibility that the Dud is not the pastor but *you yourself.*

I'm always surprised that a large number of parishioners leave the parish without even telling the pastor why or what their complaint is. I realize that speaking up can be very difficult. It is much easier to just leave and start going to another parish. My suggestion is that parishioners should not leave their parish, but speak up and confront the pastor. Tell him what, in your opinion, needs changing in the parish.

If all else fails, it may be appropriate to move on, but only after writing a letter to the bishop and personnel board, stating your reasons for changing parishes.

* * *

An Exit Strategy

When someone asks my advice about how to deal with a Fr. Dud, I recommend the following process.

• Make an appointment to meet with your pastor, but take someone with you. This will help to negate a future "he said, s/he said" standoff. Share with him what it is that you see in his leadership style (or lack thereof) that, in your opinion, needs improvement.

• If this private session fails to result in a satisfactory give-and-take dialog and a path to resolution, meet with key members your parish council (if there is one). Don't just pick people who think exactly the way you do. Your case will be stronger if you can show that you have consulted parishioners who agree with your ideas and some who might not (to add balance). Ask their support of your desired pastor-parishioner dialog.

• If you are still unable to open a two-way discussion with your pastor, contact your local bishop (your pastor's boss) and ask for an appointment.

• Another suggestion? Share this book with your pastor, after highlighting pertinent passages.

If all else fails, it may be clearly and appropriately the time to move on to a more life-giving, community-minded parish. But, *don't* leave without at least sending a letter to your bishop and priest personnel board, sharing with them your concerns about the spiritual vision and leadership of the parish you are leaving.

15

What Is the Job Description of a Bishop?

The Bishop's number one concern must be for the care and concern of parishes and parish life in his diocese. Little else matters. No one else in the Roman Catholic tradition can replace the role or position of the bishop.

So what is a bishop to do when he is surrounded by Dud-like pastors? *The bishop's job, mission and assignment must be to model and promote what parish life should be about,* in harmony with a Post-Vatican II teaching and vision. After that, he must make caring people available as pastors. This presumes the availability of caring and competent people to serve as pastors, given the present shortages of vocations and clergy.

This raises the whole question of who can be ordained today—and why or why not. For a variety of reasons, a bishop may not be able or willing to act at this point, but there is still a great deal he can do, without addressing who is ordained and who is not. In our diocese, we have had two effective examples, completely in keeping with current Canon Law.

One is Cath McGhee who was the effective acting pastor at St. Monica's for nine years. As a matter of fact, one parishioner strongly objected to her assignment there as co-pastor and even went so far as to tell the bishop that his job is to appoint priests as pastor (whether that priest is alcoholic, pedophile, or bigot). After consulting with the parish council, the bishop's response was to assign Cath as acting pastor. It is noteworthy that shortly thereafter that same parishioner became her close collaborator, advocate, and a fan. It is worthy of note that this took place, not in a small innercity parish, but in a large, growing, and affluent area.

Another example and model for our diocese was Steve Mullin, a married man, who served 12 years as pastor of a large multi-lingual and demanding parish, with two priests as acting associates. Steve brought that parish to life.

All this makes it very hard for me to agree that bishops can do nothing to change our practice and policy as a church. At the same time, a bishop might easily advocate for ordination of laity or at least the possibility of ordination of women as parish deacons. Above all, the role and concern of the bishop must focus on parish life and its wellbeing. This calls for attentive listening to parishioners' concerns and acting, if necessary, to do something about them.

In no way can or should a bishop respond to every complaint by removing or replacing pastors. At the very least, he needs to convey by his response that parish life matters and the views of parishioners are an essential part of this. Perhaps the most important thing a bishop can do is to convey by his response that parishioners' views do matter, whether it's possible for him to act on them or not.

As I said in the Foreword to this book, pastors matter and so do bishops.

CPSIA information can be obtained
at www.ICGtesting.com
Printed in the USA
LVOW01*0002080217
523498LV00017B/530/P